UNLOCKING YOUR CHILD'S GENIUS

101+ Ways To Maximize The Potential Of Your Visual Learner

Jessica L. Parnell

Discover!Press

Discover! Press, Northeast Education Associates, Catasauqua, Pennsylvania, 18032

ISBN-13: 978-0-9961361-0-5

Editorial services provided by: Deborah Crush, Kimberly Kulp
Book design: Christopher Farrell
Printed in the United States of America

101+ Ways to Maximize the Potential of Your Visual Learner

If you are the parent of a strongly Visual Learner, you can likely relate to this Mom's comment regarding her son's success in school:

"When I interact with Jeremiah, I see a kid who understands things much more deeply than others his age. He is always making connections, noticing when people are hurting, and figuring out how to fix what is broken. I see this amazingly talented and intelligent kid with so much potential. But all of that seems to change when he heads off to school. He struggles with math and can't seem to remember what he is learning in most subjects. He calls himself stupid and can't seem to say what he wants to say. It breaks my heart. How do we get him through this?"

What this Mom is seeing in her son is unfortunately the same scenario for all too many Visual Learners. They are curious, playful, and filled with wonder about the world around them. They are insightful and sensitive to the needs of others. And they are incredibly creative. These little geniuses head off to school filled with enthusiasm and excitement.

But, all too quickly, that hunger for learning begins to wane, school becomes a struggle, and their little spirits become discouraged.

So how do you combat those inevitable frustrations? What can you as a parent do to help your Visual Learner realize his or her incredible gifts and abilities and maximize potential?

This short booklet is filled with more than 101 things you need to know about your Visual Learner.

FIVE KEY THINGS TO KNOW
ABOUT YOUR VISUAL LEARNER

Visual Learners learn best by seeing what they are being taught, by watching others, and by having the opportunity to create visualizations of what they are hearing. They prefer charts, graphs, images, maps, animations, graphic organizers — basically any visual representation of what they are learning.

1. Most (but not all) Visual Learners are global learners. This means that although they understand the solution, they likely struggle or get frustrated with the steps necessary to get there. Thus, they can feel like failures in an educational system where showing your work or moving step-by-step through new material is a requirement.

2. Because they are more concerned about understanding the idea than they are about demonstrating that understanding, Visual Learners likely know much more than they show you or even realize that they know.

3. Visual Learners tend to rely on the right hemisphere — the problem solving part of the brain. They are charged and ready to go when the material is new and interesting, challenging or funny. They have little motivation when things seem irrelevant or overly simplistic. As a result they are often identified as strugglers.

4. Visual Learners literally do think, learn, and process information by creating pictures in their mind. Therefore, it is important to be aware that if they are averting their eyes, they are likely thinking and visualizing their answer. Do your best not to interrupt this process, because once interrupted, it will be difficult for them to recapture their image.

5. Your Visual Learners respond well to humor—so finding ways to keep lessons lighthearted and fun will increase their ability to connect to ideas, concepts, and new skills.

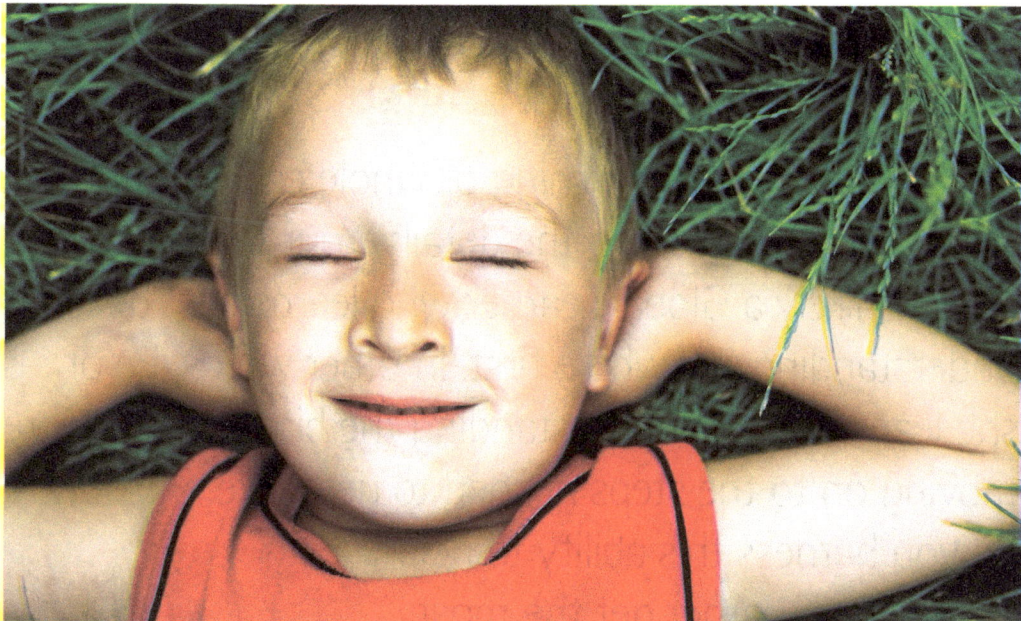

Things to Consider:

Name at least one instance when your Visual Learner knew much more than you realized.

....
....
....
....
....

My child demonstrates the following characteristics listed above:

....
....
....
....

THE BEST WAY TO PRESENT INFORMATION TO VISUAL LEARNERS

Provide the overarching or whole concept first, before explaining the details. Your Visual Learner is likely a Global Learner who learns best by understanding the whole first. In other words, he or she learns best by understanding the big picture before moving on to the steps needed to get there. So, how do you harness this ability to help your Visual Learner get the most out of learning?

Use a whole/part three-step learning model:

1. Introduce the whole first and thus provide the larger framework of the topic. This will motivate your Visual Learners and provide context for learning.

2. Next, focus on the parts; the details, expertise, and activities that make up the whole.

3. From there, go back to the whole to allow your learners to place their newly mastered skills in context.

Brainstorm a topic you are currently teaching. Jot down how you can present the whole first, then break up the various parts, then consider how you will review the whole. Take time to think it through — you'll be amazed how well things go when you plan this approach.

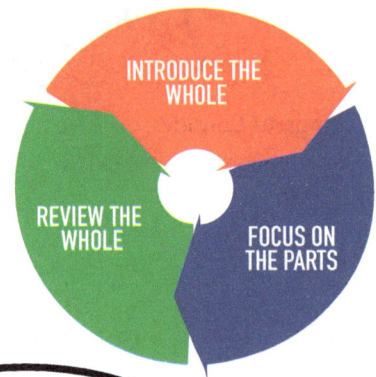

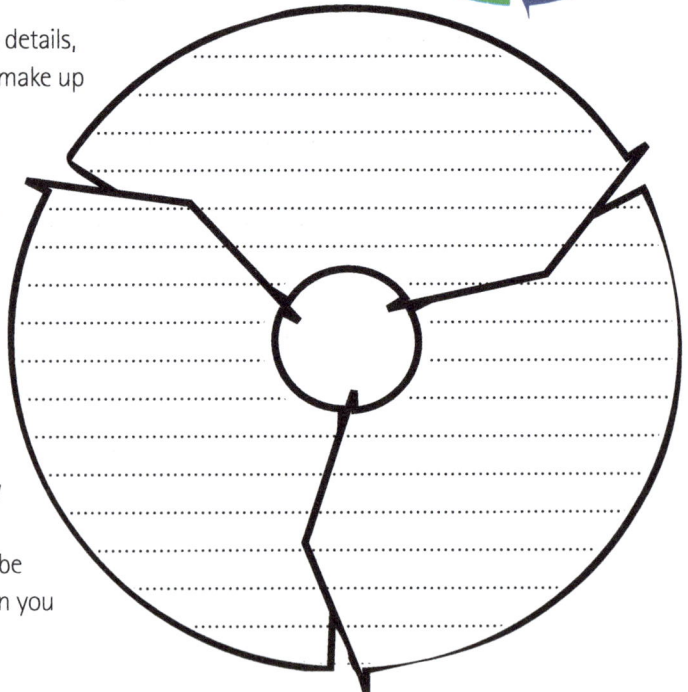

INTRODUCE THE WHOLE

FOCUS ON THE PARTS

REVIEW THE WHOLE

10 THINGS TO KEEP IN MIND WHEN MAKING EDUCATIONAL DECISIONS

Believe it or not, there are ideal environments and specific curriculum options that will appeal well to your Visual Learners. Finding that right fit can often mean the difference between struggle and success. Although you don't want to limit their input options to just the visual, teaching to their strengths in those subjects they find difficult will not only help them do well but also overcome mental blocks that often develop after repeated struggle. But it's not just about the textbook or online course you choose; read on to discover what else you should think about as you make those all-important educational decisions.

1. Visual Learners learn best when using curriculum that offers plenty of illustrations, pictures,

charts, story maps, diagrams, etc., to reinforce learning.

2. A hands-on approach to learning often works well, because Visual Learners are then able to create what they are seeing or doing in their brain.

3. Keep the environment in check. Visual Learners often overreact to or are distracted by noise. This can be tough to manage in a classroom, but essential to keeping your student engaged.

   When presenting difficult concepts do your best to do it in an environment that is not so noisy that you lose their attention. Provide a quiet place for independent reading and studying.

4. Visual Learners tend to be quite tuned in to similarities and differences and have an amazing ability to make connections. In fact, they learn best by seeing relationships between what they already know and the new information coming in. Make this part of your teaching process. After each lesson, have them process what they have learned by thinking through the following questions:

   The main point of this lesson was...
   This reminds me of...
   I would like to know more about...

5. Many times, Visual Learners are defined as perfectionists. As a result, they often struggle to complete a project or assignment because it doesn't seem worthy of turning in. But sometimes what they have already achieved is enough. Help them identify when an assignment is "good enough" and when they may need to put some more effort into it.

6. Because of their perfectionism, some Visual Learners need to be pushed to complete what they started. If this is a consistent problem with your learners, plan to select at least one project or assignment per month to take to perfection. Give some extra time to really focus and fine-tune their selection. Then, be sure to celebrate their success!

7. Visual Learners may struggle with auditory processing and communications. This means that, although they hear you talking, they often don't register the information that they take in through their ears. This can be especially frustrating if you are an auditory learner who can quickly process and retain what you hear. Keep in mind, this is often not deliberate, so be patient. If something is really important, be sure to have them jot some notes that they can come back to later.

8. Engage with them face to face — many Visual Learners need eye contact in order to focus. Be sure to grab their attention by deliberately maintaining eye contact. (A great way to do this without distracting yourself is to just look from one eye to the other — they won't even notice and it gives you something to focus on besides how awkward it feels to hold eye contact for such a long time.) On the other hand, you may notice they look to the side before responding. This is often their way of picturing what they need to say, so give them space to do so.

9. Visual Learners will struggle with multiple choice tests. Why? Because they are outstanding with analysis. As a result, they can often support all of the options in a multiple choice test and will have trouble settling on just one.

10. Good relationships are essential to learning. Keep your relationships positive and encouraging. Stay positive — your Visual Learner is very sensitive to your mood, facial expressions, and attitude.

Things to Consider:

What are three things I can do differently right now based on what I just learned?

....

....

....

....

My child has already overcome the following struggles:

....

....

....

....

10 WAYS TO HARNESS YOUR CHILD'S VISUAL STRENGTH

The great thing about strongly visual kids is their uncanny ability to picture what they are learning. Since 50% of our brain is dedicated to the visual, they tend to remember what they see better than the rest of us! In addition, our brain processes images 60,000 times faster than the written word. For these kids who are already gifted in the visual modality, seeing it means faster processing and better memory. How do you appeal to those strengths and help them realize just how incredibly well their brain works?

1. **Appeal to their love of color.** The right hemisphere thrives on color. Therefore, teaching your Visual Learner to use different color pens or markers to take notes can help them retain information. They can color code each type of information, each subject, or use alternate colors for main points and supporting ideas.

2. **Have Visual Learners prepare for tests by sketching information** rather than just reviewing text.

3. **Make colorful sticker charts to track goals,** chores, and other responsibilities.

4. **Allow them to use highlighters** as they read to identify important points and add color to the page. (This does mean they will need their own copies of text, but you will not regret it!)

5. **Provide visual activities** such as maps, videos, puzzles, models, matching activities, computers, and word games.

6. **Write things down.** Both you and your Visual Learners can take advantage of their ability to remember what they see by writing things down.

   Instructor/Parent: When giving a lot of oral instructions, a lecture, an assignment, project or deadline, **put something in writing for your student or they may forget your instructions.**

   Students: **Take every opportunity to write down assignments,** take good notes or jot yourself a reminder of what you are thinking.

7. **Give them time to form an image in their head as you present material or as they read.**
    Visual Learners can literally see the setting and the action as they read it and are, therefore, less
    likely to rush through a book. Instead, they will read slowly and form pictures in their head as
    they read. Be aware that Visual Learners often end up identified as slow readers or as having
    poor reading comprehension, because they read slowly and may not complete the reading
    in time to tackle the questions. If your students are struggling, avoid putting a time limit on
    reading comprehension activities—you will likely be amazed at what they remember when
    given the opportunity to read at their own pace.

8. **Further develop their observation skills** by taking them outside and allowing them to just
    sit and take it in. Turn it into an art project by taking along some art supplies and have them
    choose how they will capture their setting — Will they try to draw an entire scene or just focus
    on one element, like a specific plant or animal? Turn it into a descriptive writing assignment
    where they need to capture what they are seeing, hearing, smelling, and feeling around them.

9. **Allow them to doodle to stay focused.** Visual Learners process information differently and
    often have insights the rest of us miss. Giving them the ability to doodle and sketch as they
    listen keeps them focused and able to make *those amazing connections they are so good at
    seeing.* (My daughter's notebook is covered in doodles that would definitely be a distraction for
    me. But for her, doodling keeps her focused on what she is hearing and better able to retain
    and process new information.)

10. **Allow them to close their eyes and picture what they are learning** when taking in new
    information. Whether it is a word, a math problem, an event in history, a list of information or
    complex concept, allowing them the time to picture it will help transfer it to long term memory.

Questions to Consider:

Which visual strength most accurately describes your Visual Learner?

....

....

....

What strategies are you already using to harness the strength of your Visual Learner?

....

....

....

What strategy will you begin using?

....

....

....

10 TEACHING TIPS FOR YOUR VISUAL LEARNER

By now you have already identified a few things you can immediately implement to help Visual Learners realize their incredible potential. Perhaps you plan to incorporate more color into their day, or require them to do more note taking. Maybe you will focus on getting them past that mental block that often occurs due to their perfectionistic nature. You may be wondering how this all translates to your teaching? What can you do on a day-to-day basis to teach to their strengths?

Keep reading!

1. **Make it challenging.** Keeping your teaching, practice activities and assessments at a higher level will provide the motivation that helps them succeed. Select curricula that focuses on critical thinking and analysis rather than simply skill building. Don't be afraid to add extras that get them thinking or creating.

2. **Pause often when giving oral instructions.** Recognize that some Visual Learners may not have the ability to listen and write at the same time. Therefore, present new information in small snippets and pause to allow them to capture what they heard on the page before moving on.

3. **If you see your Visual Learners struggling to understand a concept, take a break and come back to it later.** Explaining it verbally over and over again from the same angle will not bring success — it will simply frustrate them. Sometimes taking a break will give their brain the time it needs to work it out. If not, have them explain it to you—you will be amazed at how much they understand.

4. **Give them advance notice when moving on to something new.** It is often difficult for Visual Learners to move on to the next thing on the schedule—especially when what they are doing involves the creative process. Giving them fair warning can help prepare them for the transition so they can quickly focus on what's next.

5. **Avoid pushing them towards drill, practice or repetition** (unless you see a real struggle). This is not an effective teaching method for your Global Learners. Instead, make the information meaningful to them. Give them opportunities to ask a lot of questions and build their framework. This will lead to a better and more permanent understanding.

6. **Demonstrate what you want your child to do first.** They learn so much more by watching than they do by hearing.

7. **Use advanced puzzles, LEGOs, mazes, etc., to harness and build their problem solving abilities.**

8. **Give lots of opportunity for creativity**—when they have the time to use their artistic and creative minds, they will amaze you. You will likely end up with something you can use to teach future students!

9. **Allow for plenty of creative writing assignments rather than just expository writing.** Visual Learners are often fantastic writers when given license to be creative. Write historical fiction stories to review a specific time period or person in history; develop a press release on a new scientific discovery; mimic the style of a specific author when studying literature – the possibilities are endless. Your Visual Learner will shine when able to approach writing with a creative mindset.

10. **Give them time to answer questions.** Remember, Visual Learners need to translate their ideas from picture to words so be patient. On the other hand, recognize they may need to just blurt out what is on their mind. Allowing them to speak before they lose their thought can make a big difference in both learning and confidence.

Things to Consider:

List three suggestions from above that you will begin to implement right now and a few ideas on what you plan to do:

1. ....

....

....

2. ....

....

....

3. ....

....

....

12 EASY-TO-USE TIPS FOR ASSESSING YOUR VISUAL LEARNER

Remember we talked about avoiding multiple choice tests because Visual Learners are so good at analysis they can defend every answer? What many learners (and teachers) find the easiest form of assessment is actually the most difficult for Visual Learners. When we limit ourselves to just this option, we often end up thinking they know much less than they do. What are some concrete ways to assess Visual Learners that will not only help them succeed but also help them transfer information more solidly into long-term memory?

Develop assessments that harness the ability to think globally. Capitalize on your Visual Learners' ability to think globally by creating assessments that focus on the bigger picture or application of information, rather than the minute details.

Tips for Creating Math Assessments that Work

11. Visual Learners are often able to find the answer in math without going through all the steps. Allow them opportunities to complete math problems in ways that play to their strengths, rather than having to show their work.

12. When studying concepts having a specific sequence that you believe is essential for them to master, have them draw a series of boxes and sketch the appropriate sequence in each box. This adds both a visual and problem solving element to the assignment that will appeal to their analytical side.

Tips for Creating Assessments in Reading and Literature – that Work.

13. Rather than have them memorize dates and details, ask questions like, "How does this story apply to your life today?" or "How did the author employ (characterization, setting, conflict, etc.) during the scene about xyz?"

14. Create a map of the settings used in the story or have them sketch out a specific scene from the story.

15. Create a movie poster for the premiere of a movie made about the book.

Tips for Creating Science Assessments that Work

16. Sketch and label a diagram. For a lesson on anatomy, have the student diagram the ear and label each part. Take this further by adding a short sentence about the function of each part and a quick analysis of what would happen if one part no longer functioned properly.

17. Create a flow chart that illustrates a process that ties in to what you are learning. For example:

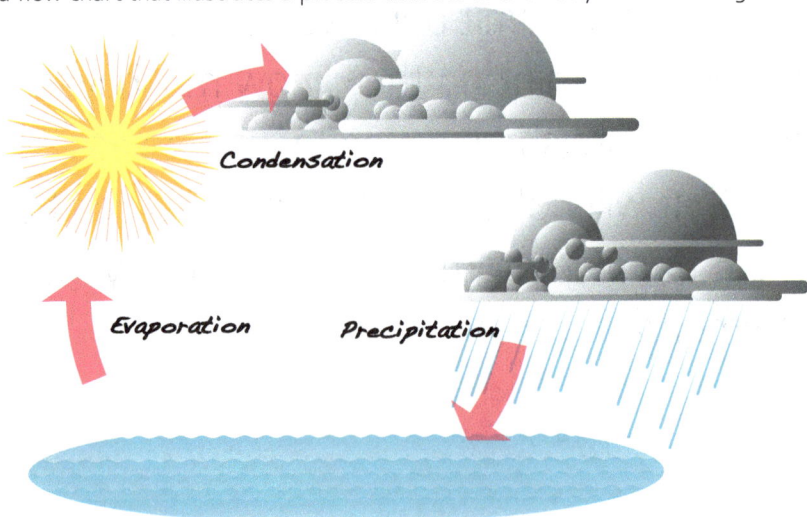

Condensation

Evaporation　　*Precipitation*

Tips for Creating History Assessments that Work

18. Rather than requiring Visual Learners to answer multiple choice questions about a time period or historical character, have them create a PPT presentation, website, Facebook profile, etc., that captures the characteristics or main points discussed.

19. Ask Visual Learners to write a journal article about a specific event or decision from the perspective of an individual in history, for example, "Capture the struggle that President Truman had in making the decision to drop the Atom bomb on the Japanese cities of Hiroshima and Nagasaki."

20. Use problem solving-assessments as often as possible. Problem solving assessments go beyond simply providing word problems in math and they include a scientific problem that needs to be resolved using principles of physics or a historical dilemma considering different events leading up to the problem. Getting these higher level thinkers engaged will energize them and make learning much more meaningful.

21. Allow extra time for testing. Because they are so good at analysis, Visual Learners tend to need extra time in a traditional test setting as they wrestle with every possible answer. That extra time can be the difference between success and discouragement, so lighten up on timed tests. After all, your goal is to assess what they know, not what they can do in a set amount of time.

Response:

Go back and highlight the assessment ideas that you plan to implement in the coming weeks and months. Make a list of other assessment ideas that you are excited to try with your Visual Learner.

....

....

....

....

....

10 WAYS TO HARNESS YOUR VISUAL LEARNER'S ABILITY TO MAKE CONNECTIONS

As explained earlier, Visual Learners have an incredible ability to make connections. They will often say things like, "That story reminds me of the time that we..." or "Don't you think this lesson is like the one we studied about...". Their brains are always working to connect new information to old.

We all do this but their connection networks tend to be supercharged and always in gear. Since they are tuned in to analyzing similarities and differences, gearing your presentation of new material to that strength will help them better understand and make long-lasting connections.

Visual Learners learn best by seeing relationships. If you can connect new information to old as you present, do so. Or, ask older learners to demonstrate the relationship as part of their synthesis of new information. Here are a few ways you can help them make connections as they gather new information in various subject areas.

MATH

1. **Have them list or sketch out how a new concept builds on another.** For example, discuss how learning to add and subtract fractions relies on the skills of addition, subtraction and multiplication. If simplifying, help them make the connection to the skill of division.

2. **Use fraction circle manipulatives** to show how fractions fit into one another as well as the larger circle.

3. **Stack up decimals** to compare and contrast the base-ten place value system.

LANGUAGE ARTS

4. **Grammar** — Make the connection between grammar lessons and writing by having students identify the subject nouns, adjectives, adverbs, and prepositions in their own writing. You will be amazed at how much easier grammar becomes when they can connect it to what they are doing.

5. **Writing**—Give samples of good writing to emulate in their own paragraphs, essays, and compositions. Helping them see examples of what works gives them the visual framework they need to do the same.

6. **Reading and Literature.** Make personal connections to the characters, lessons, plot of the story, etc., with questions like:

   "Which character is most like you and why?"

   "What lesson or theme in the book can you apply directly to your life?"

   "Can you think of a time when you had to learn the same lesson that <main character> did?"

   "What events in this story remind you of events in your own life or in history?"

SCIENCE

7. **Consider the relationship between living things and their environment.** What specific parts of their habitat help them to thrive?

8. **Create a comparison chart or Venn Diagram** to analyze.

SOCIAL STUDIES

9. **When studying world history,** you can help them connect civilizations through compare and contrast.

GEOGRAPHY

10. Map out the changes in geography as various civilizations or world powers claim and reclaim land.

Sample World History Assignment

As we have learned, both sides of the Great War believed that World War I would bring a quick and easy victory. They did not expect it to last for years and were not quite prepared for such a long and brutal war. Use the information we have studied to analyze the powers on both sides at the start of the war.

THE CENTRAL POWERS: GERMANY AND AUSTRIA-HUNGARY	
STRENGTHS	WEAKNESSES

THE ALLIED POWERS: GREAT BRITAIN, FRANCE, ITALY, RUSSIA	
STRENGTHS	WEAKNESSES

Things to Consider:

Compare and contrast your current approach to each subject listed with the suggestions on the previous pages. Use a green marker or pen to underline the ideas you want to implement.

Subject	Current Approach/Textbook	Suggested Approach
Math		
Language Arts		
Science		
Social Studies		

4 EASY WAYS TO BUILD TIME MANAGEMENT SKILLS

A Visual or Spatial Learner often struggles with deadlines, time management, and overall timeliness. This can be a frustration for the whole family. As you know, time management is essential for success as adults — we are accountable to schedules and deadlines established by our spouse, boss, co-workers, coaches, etc. A great way to build this skill is to establish manageable expectations and allow your child to take ownership of them. Help them manage their time by creating a schedule and helping them stick to it. Turn the page for a few simple ways to teach time management and responsibility.

1. **Make lists to develop independence.** If you are looking for them to be independent in their learning, provide a list or weekly planner they can follow and manage on their own. If you are a Bridgeway Academy student, allow them to manage their own Instructor's Guide for each course (but do check in to ensure they are on track).

2. **Map out deadlines and create step–by–step deadlines for reaching their goal.** You can even make this appeal to their visual strengths by mapping it out on a timeline. Then, be sure to check in often to hold them to it!

3. **If being on time is important, set the alarm** on their phone or watch to give them a 5, 10 or 15 minute warning and keep them on track for getting there on time.

4. **Give them 10 minutes every morning to look at their day and chart out how they will tackle their various responsibilities and commitments.** An easy to use chart like the one below gives them ownership of their own time and rewards them for completion every time they finish a task (that simple check mark goes a long way). This not only helps them stick to it but also teaches responsibility and good time management skills. Below are two ways you can organize their chart—select the one that best fits your family.

Time of Day	Subject/Task	Anticipated Time Needed	Done
Morning	*Math*	*30 min.*	✔
8:30–9:00	*English*	*30 min.*	

8 POTENTIAL STRUGGLES FOR VISUAL LEARNERS

No parent or teacher of a Visual Learner needs me to outline the potential struggles for Visual Learners. In fact, you can probably add to this list, and I encourage you to do so. Despite their incredible gifts, Visual Learners experience struggles as they navigate academics and daily life. Helping them deal with those struggles and frustrations makes them stronger learners and more confident individuals. Be aware of how you can help and encourage them to think differently. At the end of this chapter you can create your action plan. Think beyond what you see here as you create your plan to help unlock the incredible potential of your Visual Learner.

1. **Many times Visual Learners have hyper sensitive senses.** Sounds can be distracting as can be bright lights, excessive visual aids posted around the room, etc. Talk with your students to find out if there are things in their learning environment that bother their senses and find a place where they can work without distractions.

2. **Visual Learners can also be sensory avoiders who are bothered by itchy fabrics, powerful smells, tags on their clothing, seams in their socks, wide swings in temperature, and even people standing too closely.** Be willing to stop everything and get rid of what is bothering them so that learning can continue.

3. **Many Visual Learners have a high energy level and need to move their body in order think, learn and communicate well.** If your student is one of these movers and shakers, fill his or her school box with plenty of objects that get their bodies engaged as they learn. Be sure to offer plenty of breaks when they can run off some energy.

4. **Your Visual Learner responds very well to encouragement because it helps to elevate their positive emotions.** However, they have a hard time accepting criticism, even when it is meant to help them improve. As a result, learning can come to a stand still as a result of constructive criticism. Be sure to time your feedback carefully.

5. **You can harness their emotional need by seeking ways to build them up** and by finding ways to appeal to their emotions in order to help them learn.

6. **Your Visual Learner can also sense disapproval.** Often they assume your disapproval is directed at them. This can often cause them to lose focus on learning as they worry. Help them overcome this by allowing them to voice their concerns when they sense disapproval or become stressed by those around them.

7. **Despite their creative ability and artistic skills, many Visual Learners have poor handwriting skills.** This is often because their brain is thinking faster than they can write. Giving them the freedom to use a keyboard for writing assignments or short answers helps unleash those thoughts.

8. **Your Visual Learner can excel at complex concepts and learning.** However they may struggle with simple facts and sequential mastery based learning. They can be quickly frustrated by their inability to "keep up" with the students around them. If you miss this, you can quickly have a student who is turned off by learning and develops a poor self esteem, calling his/herself "dumb" or "stupid." Don't miss this! When you have a student capable of so much, simplistic learning can cripple development. Find curriculum that offers many opportunities for analytical thinking and problem solving.

Use the chart below to list the struggles you have seen in your child. Then make a list of ways you can help him/her overcome those struggles.

Struggle:

How I Can Help:

Struggle:

How I Can Help:

Struggle:

How I Can Help:

Struggle:

How I Can Help:

Struggle:

How I Can Help:

8 PROVEN WAYS TO DEVELOP
OTHER LEARNING STYLES

By now you are likely so excited about the gifts and abilities of your Visual Learner that the thought of developing other modalities is not even a concern. They are great problem solvers, have amazing insight, process and remember what they see incredibly well, and make connections many of us miss. In addition, they are often strong kinesthetic learners. The ability to create with their hands means taking what they see in their mind and illustrating it with a concrete activity. However, a strongly Visual Learner may struggle with auditory processing and communication, which is so essential in this highly verbal society.

Here are just a few strategies to help build the auditory modality and set them up for even more success in both academics and life.

1. **Storytelling is a great way to build your Visual Learner's auditory processing skills.** Stories allow students to engage their visual strengths while building listening skills.

2. **Get them involved in a discussion**. Strongly Visual Learners don't often jump into conversations easily. But once you get them involved, you will see that they have some amazing things to say. Draw them into discussion with specific questions that cannot be answered in just a few words.

3. **Grab an easy-to-read children's book** (no matter their age) and have them read it with drama and expression.

4. **Listen to audio books or audio dramas.** Some great options include: Adventures in Odyssey, Your Story Hour, Jonathan Parks, Focus on the Family Radio Theatre, Down Gilead Lane, etc.

5. **Debate is another great way to get your Visual Learner to engage listening and communication skills.** When possible, take another stance on an issue and keep them engaged in defending their position. If your Visual Learner has trouble listening, grab an object and require the speaker to be holding the object before speaking. This helps build self control and creates an environment for listening well.

6. **Capitalize on their observation skills while building communication skills.** Create a descriptive writing activity by taking them outside and allowing them sit quietly to listen to and observe their surroundings. Then have them capture that setting in words on a page.

7. **Help them understand the value of their observation skills by creating a scenario where they have to use them.** The writing activity described in the box on the right is one activity I have used many times, both in the classroom and with homeschool groups.

One of my favorite writing lessons taught was with a small home school workshop group. Two weeks prior to the lesson on descriptive writing, I brought in a sword we had purchased in Portugal. We were working on persuasive writing at the time and I explained I would be writing about why I believed police officers should go back to carrying swords (I know, tough to defend). I made a big deal about how valuable my "antique" sword was and asked that they help me remember to take it home after class. On the week designated for descriptive writing, I asked a young man to "break into" my classroom, push me aside, grab the sword and run, which he did beautifully. I, of course, was devastated by the theft and asked the class to help me describe the individual to the police. It was amazing how differently each student remembered that burglar. After the exercise, we brought him back into the room and they compared their descriptions with the actual culprit. It was a great way to have them put the observations into words, and to build up those Visual Learners.

Things to Consider:

Think through ways you have seen your Visual Learner struggle with auditory processing and memory. Write down a few concrete examples.

....

....

....

....

....

What strategies will I use to build my Visual Learner's auditory modality?

....

....

....

....

....

10 WAYS TO HELP VISUAL LEARNERS PREPARE FOR READING

For a Visual Learner, phonemic awareness will not come as naturally as it will for an auditory learner. Therefore, the younger they are when you start these suggestions, the better. Read often, be upbeat about words, and introduce letters and letter sounds with fun games and activities. Use the strategies listed here to create an environment where reading and communication are natural, exciting and fun. By the time you begin a formal introduction of reading and phonics they will be ready and eager to become independent readers.

1. **Read aloud as often as possible;** even as they grow and become independent readers.

2. **Read anything and everything;** don't limit yourself to what has been identified as appropriate for your child's age.

3. As you teach reading, put your finger under the word so they can visualize the connection between what is written and what you are saying.

4. **Encourage memorization** — memorize poems, children's stories, scripture, etc., to get the mind engaged in word processing and memory.

5. **Point out printed words as you go about your day:** Traffic signs, street names, headlines, signs in stores, words on cereal boxes and other products in stores, television ads, etc.

6. **Tell stories often.** My kids loved to hear stories about my life as well as stories where they were the main character. Get them involved as well—start the story and have them add to it.

7. **Compile books of stories they write.** We used to start with a picture from a magazine. I would paste it into their book and have them dictate a sentence or story about the pictures. This not only builds reading readiness but helps children see themselves as writers.

8. Purchase or check out books without words from the library and let them "read" the story to you.

9. **Record your children's stories** and let them listen again and again. Then transcribe those recordings and create a writing portfolio for your child.

10. **Buy rhythmic books** that make it easy for your child to memorize what you are reading. Then have them read along with you.

Things to Consider:

What strategies are you already using to get your Visual Learner excited about reading?

....

....

How can you involve siblings in these strategies?

....

....

List two to three favorite children's books that you can begin reading every day in order to build their memory until they can "read" it to you.

....

....

16 SUBJECT SPECIFIC WAYS TO ENGAGE VISUAL LEARNERS

Now, let's put it all together. If you reach this section, you have evaluated what is working, what you want to change, and ways you can help maximize the potential of your Visual Learner. You have already identified some teaching strategies you plan to implement and are excited about the possibilities. The ideas listed in this section are concrete ways you can appeal to the strengths of your Visual Learner as you teach different subjects and skills. So go ahead, grab an idea, test it, and find out what works best for your individual learner. Then, keep going—you both will have fun discovering new ways to teach and learn!

LANGUAGE ARTS

1. **Encourage students to notice descriptive words and details as they read.** For them, the details and descriptions make stories come alive. Once they recognize the technique, they can apply it to their own writing.

2. Allow them to use a **keyboard** for writing and responding.

3. **Allow them to see their spelling words one at a time** before asking them to spell them (pre-tests don't work well with Visual Learners because once they have spelled it incorrectly, their brain has visualized it incorrect.)

4. **Many Visual Learners will struggle with d and b, q and p.** A great way to help with this is have them color code the letters as they write and practice using them in words. By picturing the color coded words, they can draw upon their visual strengths when taking a spelling test.

5. **Use pre-writing techniques** that allow your learners to create a visual to work from as they write.

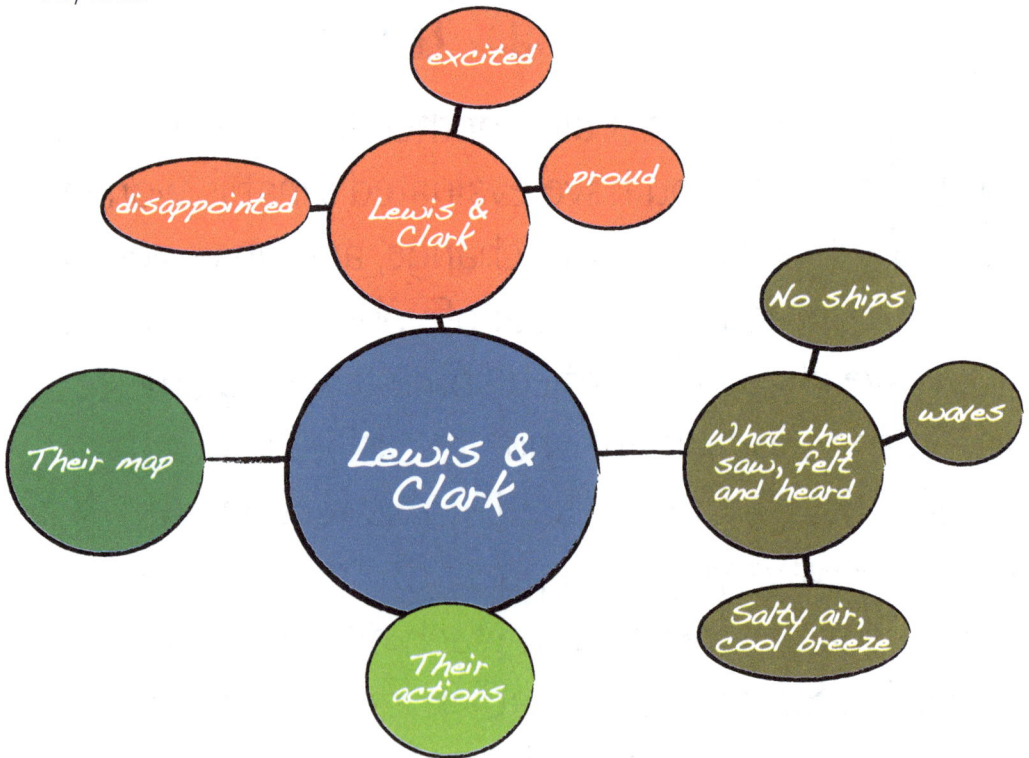

MATH

6. **Look for an approach that focuses on mathematical thinking and reasoning rather than computation.** Singapore Math is a terrific example and is both strongly visual and analytical.

7. **Use flashcards when memorizing.**

8. Although they may struggle with math computation and memorizing multiplication tables, **these students will excel in geometry, trigonometry, calculus, and advanced algebra.**

9. **Use manipulatives and pictures to demonstrate math concepts.**

10. **Help them see how everything fits together the first time you explain it.** For example, when presenting fractions, use pictures or real objects to show how each part fits into the whole.

Fraction of a whole

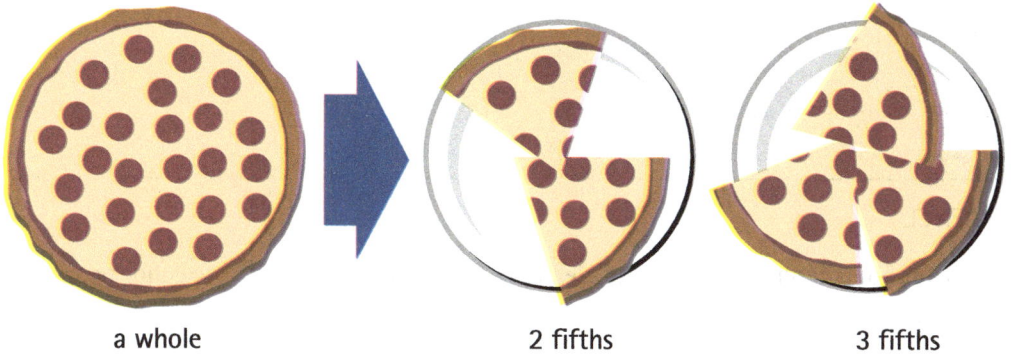

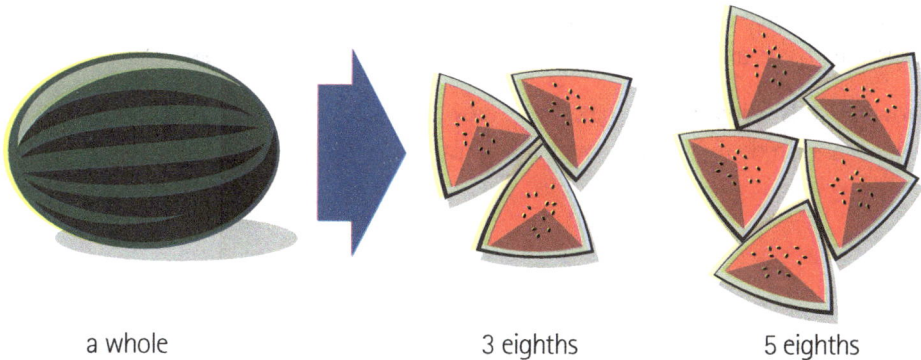

a whole	2 fifths	3 fifths

Fraction of a whole

a whole	3 eighths	5 eighths

SOCIAL STUDIES

11. **Use historical fiction to make history come alive.**

12. **Connect time periods, leaders, wars, and developments by creating Venn Diagrams or T-Charts** that allow them to compare and contrast and evaluate how one event, leader or country may have affected another.

	EGYPTIAN	SUMERIAN
What river system did each civilization depend on for food?	Nile	Tigris and Euphrates
Both found ways to communicate in writing. What was their form of writing?	Picture Writing— hieroglyphics	Picture Writing— cuneiform
Both built great monuments that are still seen today. What were they called?	Pyramids	Ziggurats

SCIENCE

13. **Offer opportunities for discovery learning** through experiments, the scientific process, architecture projects, science collections, etc.

14. **Find ways to let them use their mechanical gifts;** building something, taking things apart to see how they work, designing, etc.

15. **Download a blank calendar for the month** and track the **phases of the moon** by drawing the moon you see out your window every night. After you are done, have your student name the phases and calculate the number of days between each phase.

16. **Grow crystals using Borax.** The crystals grow very quickly – about one day. Hang them in a window and study them with a magnifying glass.

Try this fun experiment for kids of all ages to see just how much power can be found in the air we breathe.

You Will Need:

☐ 1 balloon

☐ 1 straw

☐ 1 long piece of string that measures 10-15 ft. long (kite string works best)

☐ Tape

Step-by-Step Instructions

1. Tie one end of the string to a stationary object (chair, door knob, etc.).

2. Place the other end of the string through the straw, pull the string tightly to connect to another stationary object.

3. Fill the balloon with air, pinching the end of the balloon rather than tying it.

4. Tape the balloon to the straw allowing the balloon to fall below the straw and string line.

5. Release the air from the balloon and watch the balloon launch along the string!

Things to Consider

1. What made the balloon move along the string line?

....

2. Do you think the shape of the balloon had any effect on the movement of the balloon?

....

3. What would help the balloon move faster or slower along the string line?

....

4. Does the angle of the string have any effect on how far or fast the balloon travels?

....

10 TIPS AND TOOLS YOU CAN USE AS A VISUAL LEARNER

We've covered a lot of ideas and strategies for parents and teachers to try as they work with Visual Learners. In this chapter we shift to strategies that you can use if you yourself are a Visual Learner.

Share this chapter with your students and challenge them to take ownership of how they can use their strengths to better succeed in everything they do. Be sure to have them highlight what strategies work best and even make a list of additional ideas that they know work well.

1. **Use color as often as possible.** Use colored pens, highlighters, markers, etc. as you read, write or type. This will engage the right hemisphere that you naturally depend on and help with understanding and long term retention.

2. **Stay on top of the lecture by predicting where the speaker is going.**

3. **Ask the following questions** as you listen to the teaching of others and record your answers.

   What is his/her main point?

   What are the important facts?

   If I were writing the test, what questions would I ask?

> *If you are a Bridgeway Academy online student, be sure to use the exclusive note taking guide to help evaluate these questions while watching the instruction online.*

4. **Take notes in pictures rather than always using words.**

5. **Create graphs and diagrams** or connect ideas through arrows, boxes, and charts so you can revisit and expand those connections later.

6. **Use stress relievers to keep yourself engaged while listening.** Adding a bit of activity can really make the difference between feeling distracted and staying focused—especially when the teaching is mostly lecture or discussion.

7. **Take the time you need to respond to questions**—especially when engaged in a verbal conversation. Too often, Visual Learners feel less than adequate because their parents or teachers who may be much more auditory are better able to keep a conversation moving.

8. **Slow down a conversation with simple statements** like, "Yes, let me think about that for a moment before I respond" or "That reminds me of something—hold on—let me pull that up in my mind" or "Ah! I get what you are saying but let me challenge you with something else."

9. **Recognize those times when you feel the need to just blurt out an answer or idea.** Use a small notebook or your cell phone to capture those ideas while they are fresh in your mind. When you find yourself interrupting or blurting out what is on your mind, recognize that this can be frustrating for others, so be careful not to be offended by their reactions.

Unlocking Your Child's Genius

10. If you will be listening to a lecture, sermon, or conference where information will be mostly auditory, request an overview first. This will help you understand the big picture before you have to listen to the details.

Reflection for Visual Learners:

Starting now, I am going to use this strategy as I approach learning:

....

....

....

How will I use this strategy?

....

....

....

Think back to a time when you approached learning using one of your visual strengths. What was the outcome? Can you explain what happened when you shifted to using this strength?

....

....

....

FINAL COMMENTS

Before you close the book, let me encourage you to think back on what we have covered. Consider any new insights or ideas, strategies or teaching tips you plan to implement. Think through what you have discovered about your amazing Visual Learners, then use this space to jot a note of appreciation and encouragement. Tell what you love, what gifts you see and what ways you hope to encourage them. Let them know they inspire you and what gifts you would like to help understand and develop. Make a commitment: What do you intend to do differently or to keep doing that will help maximize their potential? This little exercise will not only help you to process all you have learned but will be a fantastic way to share it with your children.